Theme from
"SCHINDLER'S LIST"

From the Universal Motion Picture SCHINDLER'S LIST

Cello and Piano

JOHN WILLIAMS

ISBN 978-1-4950-7162-1

Visit Hal Leonard Online at
www.halleonard.com

HAL•LEONARD®

7777 W. BLUEMOUND RD. P.O. BOX 13819 MILWAUKEE, WI 53213

With the creation of his 1993 film *Schindler's List*, I have always felt that Steven Spielberg has given us a genuine masterpiece. With its penetrating portrayal of Oskar Schindler's heroic rescue of hundreds of Holocaust victims, the film delivers a powerful moral message for generations of viewers.

The original score for the film included a memorable performance by violinist Itzhak Perlman playing the main musical theme. For many years, I have thought that cellists might also bring their own particular magic to this music, and I am proud to offer this adaptation that I have made expressly for them.

Theme from
"SCHINDLER'S LIST"

From the Universal Motion Picture SCHINDLER'S LIST

Cello and Piano

JOHN WILLIAMS

SOLO CELLO

Theme from
"SCHINDLER'S LIST"

From the Universal Motion Picture SCHINDLER'S LIST

Cello and Piano

J O H N   W I L L I A M S

ISBN 978-1-4950-7162-1

Visit Hal Leonard Online at
www.halleonard.com

7777 W. BLUEMOUND RD. P.O. BOX 13819 MILWAUKEE, WI 53213

Theme from
"SCHINDLER'S LIST"

From the Universal Motion Picture SCHINDLER'S LIST

Cello and Piano

JOHN WILLIAMS

SOLO CELLO

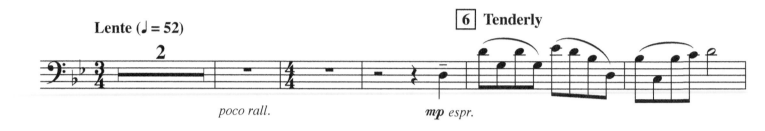

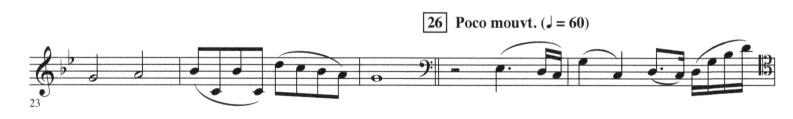

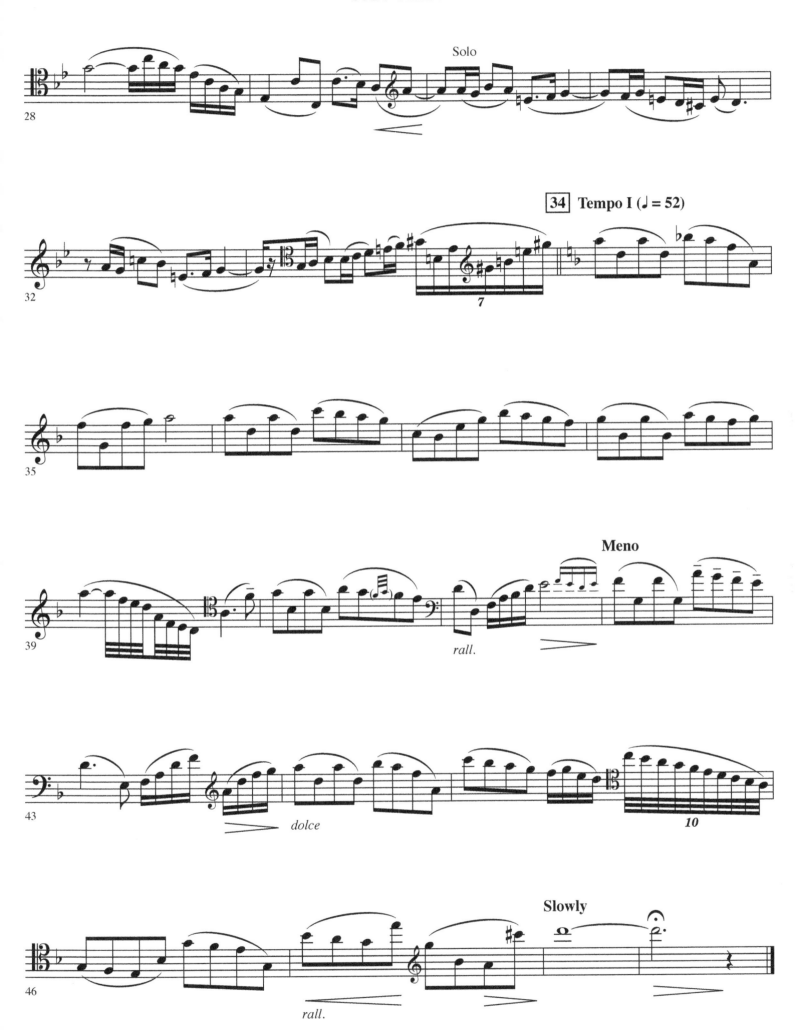